Apple Tree Fa...

the highest point
of the track

the old track

Published in the United States by Clarkson N. Potter, Inc., 225 Park Avenue South,
New York, New York 10003, and represented in Canada by the Canadian MANDA Group

Originally published in Great Britain by Macdonald and Co. (Publishers) Ltd. as
Bellamy's Changing World: The Roadside

CLARKSON N. POTTER, POTTER, and colophon are trademarks of Clarkson N. Potter, Inc.

Conceived, edited, and designed by Frances Lincoln Limited
Design and Art Direction Debbie MacKinnon

Manufactured in Italy
Library of Congress and Cataloging-in-Publication Data

Bellamy, David J.
The roadside.
(Our changing world)
Summary: Describes how the construction of a six-lane
highway in a wilderness area disrupts the balance of nature
and forces the animals there to struggle for existence.
1. Roadside ecology—Juvenile literature. 2. Man—
Influence on nature—Juvenile literature. [1. Roadside
ecology. 2. Ecology. 3. Man—Influence on nature] I. Dow, Jill, ill.
II. Title. III. Series: Bellamy, David J. Our changing world.
QH541.5.R62B45   1988   574.5'264   88-5792
ISBN 0-517-56976-0

10 9 8 7 6 5 4 3 2 1
First American Edition

O U R
C H A N G I N G
W O R L D

The
ROADSIDE

by **DAVID BELLAMY**

with illustrations by Jill Dow

Clarkson N. Potter, Inc./Publishers
DISTRIBUTED BY CROWN PUBLISHERS, INC., NEW YORK

It's midsummer and the countryside is bright with wildflowers. Just off the main road a wheat field and an old farm track meet at this gate. Soon, machinery will be brought in to harvest the wheat and take it away to store. The track is rarely used. It leads to Apple Tree Farm, but the big company that farms the land doesn't use the buildings.

The farmhouse is deserted, and the partly overgrown
track is a perfect home for all sorts of wildlife. Butterflies
and other insects feed on the nectar of the ox-eye
daisies, chicory, purple knapweed, and vetch.
A vole pokes its head out of a can that
has been carelessly thrown away.

Farther on, where the old track goes through the woods, ferns and mosses nestle in the damp coolness beneath the trees. A toad sits motionless on a stone. In places, the ruts in the track have filled with rainwater and marsh marigolds and rushes grow around them. The fallen trunk of a silver birch is full of holes made by woodpeckers searching for insects, and clusters of bracket fungi are growing on the dead wood. A fox hurries away around the corner. He has to be careful when people are about.

Just beyond the woods the foxes have their den under a hedgerow of sweet chestnut and dog-rose bushes. With only the cows looking on, the vixen rolls in the loose earth and the dog fox sniffs cautiously at a large toad which he has disturbed from its resting place. He knows the toad has a bad taste and that he'd better stick to eating rabbits, birds, rats, and mice, if he can catch them. Though all is quiet here now, the foxes have to watch out for danger. A track like this is popular with hunters with guns.

Farther down, a stream runs across the track and into the pond in the field beyond. The great willow tree likes the damp, so do the cattails and the reeds growing at the edge of the water. It's very quiet today.

A fish jumps and startles the heron. The otters playing on the other side of the pond look up too. After some rain, young toads have come out to sit on the waterlily leaves, while the old toad tries in vain to catch a large dragonfly. In the reeds a pair of reed warblers is also looking for insects to eat.

As the track winds up the hill it runs close to more of the farm company's neat fields. The edge by the old track is overgrown with tall yellow goldenrod, pink spears of fireweed, and clumps of mauve asters and below them, poppies, ragwort, and sunspurge. A flock of sparrows feeds on the seeds. Some harvest mice have woven a nest among the barley stalks, and the dog fox hunts along the far side of the field.

From the highest part of the track there is a fine view of the surrounding countryside with big new grain silos in the distance. Here the track passes around an outcrop of sandstone where butterflies sun their wings and banded snails cluster on nearby plants.

A thrush has been feeding, using a flat stone on which to smash open the shells of the snails it likes to eat. Owl pellets lie on another stone. That tawny owl flying over the fields in the late afternoon may rest here between meals. One of the pellets he coughed up has broken open. It is full of all the indigestible parts, like the fur and bones, of the mice and voles he fed on.

From around the corner, where blackberries, red campion, and Queen Anne's lace flank the track, you can see down to the old farm at last. But far from being deserted, today it seems to be a center of activity.

At the bottom of the hill a surveyor stands with a special measuring instrument called a theodolite, checking the rise

of the land all the way up to another instrument at the top. He is planning to build a highway. The peaceful old farm is about to be disturbed; already the swallows that nested in the ruined buildings are flying away, and the tawny owl's home in the dead tree may not last long either.

By the following spring the old track has turned into a sea of mud. Most of the plants and creatures have disappeared and only rushes flourish in the wheel ruts.

This is where the pond used to be. The toads, unable to find their usual spawning place, have chosen one of these puddles to lay their strings of eggs. But will the eggs have a chance to hatch? The foxes are exploring the huge drainpipes that lie on the track.

By summer, despite the ongoing upheaval all around, some plants and animals have made themselves at home. Today is Sunday and there are no workers about. Sparrows peck at the watchman's sandwiches when he goes into his hut, starlings perch boldly by the steps, and one of the foxes searches for tidbits in the trash bags. The raw mound of earth is already covered with new growth. Flowers like shepherd's purse, goldenrod, and bright blue cornflowers, which grow quickly from seed in the disturbed soil, attract the butterflies, and the ragwort is covered with caterpillars.

At last the men's work is finished. Where the old track used to wind, a straight, six-lane highway is ready for traffic. The hedgerows are gone, but the woods are still there, and the verges are seeded with grass and summer flowers that feed the butterflies again.

A kestrel hunts for mice and voles at the side of the road, and at night maybe even the owl will return. Along the highway divider ragwort and cranesbill with its pointed seed capsules are flourishing. In between, inky cap mushrooms have sprung up after last night's rain.

The road builders have done a good job. They have laid a pipe under the road to carry the stream to a big new pond on the other side. The pipe also gives the toads a safe way through from their home in the woods to their mating grounds in the pond. The reed warblers may return to the pond soon, but sadly, there is no sign of the otters, not even their footprints or their droppings, or of the heron. Perhaps there are no fish yet for them to eat.

The banks of the pond still look a bit bare, but reeds and water plants are beginning to grow at the edges and a pair of ducks is rearing its first batch of ducklings. The road doesn't seem to bother them, or the swallows, back again for another summer. In time, perhaps all kinds of plants and wildlife will be flourishing here again.

the new road

the new pond